*To:*

*From:*

*This coupon book is my gift to you to thank you for being my friend and lover. These coupons never expire and are redeemable at any time by me.*

# LOVE

## COUPONS

Gregory J.P. Godek

bestselling author of *1001 Ways to Be Romantic*

CASABLANCA PRESS
A DIVISION OF SOURCEBOOKS, INC.
NAPERVILLE, IL

Published by: Sourcebooks, Inc., P.O. Box 372, Naperville, Illinois 60566 (630) 961-3900 FAX: (630) 961-2168

Internal design and production by Andrew Sardina and Scott Theisen.

Library of Congress Cataloging-in-Publication Data
Godek, Gregory J.P.
    Love Coupons / by Gregory J.P. Godek.
        p. cm.—( A Casablanca book )
    1. Man-woman relationships—Miscellanea. 2. Intimacy (Psychology)—Miscellanea. 3. Love—Miscellanea. I. Title. II. Series.
HQ801.G555 1997
306.7—dc21                                                                                                    96-50432
                                                                                                                      CIP

Printed and bound in the United States of America.
10 9 8 7 6 5

# L♡VE

## C O U P O N S

This coupon entitles the holder to one Weekend Getaway! Here's the deal: You get to choose the weekend, and the coupon-issuer gets to choose the location.

*Personal notes* _____

_____

# "The anticipation is often as much fun as the gift or gesture itself."

-Gregory J.P. Godek, Author of *1001 Ways to Be Romantic*

- Get a free 1 year subscription to Greg Godek's *LoveLetter Newsletter*.
  Send your name and address to: LoveLetter, P.O. Box 313, Naperville, IL 60566
- Look for these books by "America's Romance Coach," Gregory J.P. Godek: *1001 Ways to Be Romantic*
  *Romantic Mischief* ~ *Romantic Fantasies* ~ *Romantic Dates* ~ *Romantic Questions*
- Check out the "World of Romance" page on the Internet: http://www.godek.com

This coupon entitles the holder to one candlelight dinner (with the issuer of the coupon) at the most romantic restaurant in town!

*Personal notes* _____

_____

# "Romance is the process... love is the goal."

-Gregory J.P. Godek, Author of *1001 Ways to Be Romantic*

This is a **Sex-Sex-Sex** coupon! The coupon giver promises to fulfill one sexual fantasy of the coupon holder's choosing. Participants must be at least 18 years of age.

*Personal notes* _____

_____

# "Romance resides in the everyday."

-Gregory J.P. Godek, Author of *1001 Ways to Be Romantic*

* Get a free 1 year subscription to Greg Godek's *LoveLetter Newsletter*.
  Send your name and address to: LoveLetter, P.O. Box 313, Naperville, IL  60566
* Look for these books by "America's Romance Coach," Gregory J.P. Godek: *1001 Ways to Be Romantic*
  *Romantic Mischief* * *Romantic Fantasies* * *Romantic Dates* * *Romantic Questions*
* Check out the "World of Romance" page on the Internet: http://www.godek.com

*This coupon entitles the holder to ... flowers! Your choice: One dozen of any kind of flower. Flowers to be delivered within 3 days of issuance of coupon.*

*Personal notes* _____

_____

"Love doesn't teach, it shows the way.
Love doesn't lecture, it just loves!"

-Gregory J.P. Godek, Author of *1001 Ways to Be Romantic*

- Get a free 1 year subscription to Greg Godek's *LoveLetter Newsletter*.
  Send your name and address to: LoveLetter, P.O. Box 313, Naperville, IL 60566
- Look for these books by "America's Romance Coach," Gregory J.P. Godek: *1001 Ways to Be Romantic*
  *Romantic Mischief* ~ *Romantic Fantasies* ~ *Romantic Dates* ~ *Romantic Questions*
- Check out the "World of Romance" page on the Internet: http://www.godek.com

This coupon entitles the holder to one sensuous backrub, performed by the issuer of the coupon. Time limit: No less than 30 minutes in duration!

*Personal notes* _____
_____

"Romance is a state of mind. It's not so much what you do as how you do it."

-Gregory J.P. Godek, Author of *1001 Ways to Be Romantic*

❧ Get a free 1 year subscription to Greg Godek's *LoveLetter Newsletter*.
   Send your name and address to: LoveLetter, P.O. Box 313, Naperville, IL  60566
❧ Look for these books by "America's Romance Coach," Gregory J.P. Godek: *1001 Ways to Be Romantic*
   *Romantic Mischief* ❧ *Romantic Fantasies* ❧ *Romantic Dates* ❧ *Romantic Questions*
❧ Check out the "World of Romance" page on the Internet: http://www.godek.com

# L♡VE

### C O U P O N S

Breakfast in bed.
Redeemable on any
day of your choosing,
sometime within the
next year.

*Personal notes* _____

_____

"Romance is a state of being. It's about taking action on your feelings of love."

-Gregory J.P. Godek, Author of *1001 Ways to Be Romantic*

**LOVE**
C O U P O N S

*This is a "Romantic ABCs Coupon." You choose one letter of the alphabet. The coupon-giver will create a day of romance with gifts and gestures that all begin with that letter.*

*Personal notes* _____

_____

"Romance is the recognition that love in the abstract has no real meaning at all."

-Gregory J.P. Godek, Author of *1001 Ways to Be Romantic*

- Get a free 1 year subscription to Greg Godek's *LoveLetter Newsletter*.
  Send your name and address to: LoveLetter, P.O. Box 313, Naperville, IL  60566
- Look for these books by "America's Romance Coach," Gregory J.P. Godek: *1001 Ways to Be Romantic*
  *Romantic Mischief* ❧ *Romantic Fantasies* ❧ *Romantic Dates* ❧ *Romantic Questions*
- Check out the "World of Romance" page on the Internet: http://www.godek.com

LOVE
C O U P O N S

**The Ultimate
Bubblebath Coupon!
You are entitled to one luxurious
bubblebath...complete with
scented bath oils, soft music,
champagne and candles.
Plus...One sensual toweling-off by
the coupon-issuer.**

*Personal notes* _____

_____

# "Romance is a bridge between the sexes."

-Gregory J.P. Godek, Author of *1001 Ways to Be Romantic*

- ❧ Get a free 1 year subscription to Greg Godek's *LoveLetter Newsletter*.
  Send your name and address to: LoveLetter, P.O. Box 313, Naperville, IL 60566
- ❧ Look for these books by "America's Romance Coach," Gregory J.P. Godek: *1001 Ways to Be Romantic*
  *Romantic Mischief* ❧ *Romantic Fantasies* ❧ *Romantic Dates* ❧ *Romantic Questions*
- ❧ Check out the "World of Romance" page on the Internet: http://www.godek.com

**L♥VE**

C O U P O N S

**This coupon entitles the holder to an *entire* weekend of romance! What's your pleasure?? The issuer of this coupon will grant your every wish! (Aladdin never had it so good!)**

*Personal notes* _____

_____

"Romance is the appreciation of two people who are celebrating the lucky coincidence that they found each other."

-Gregory J.P. Godek, Author of *1001 Ways to Be Romantic*

❧ Get a free 1 year subscription to Greg Godek's *LoveLetter Newsletter*.
Send your name and address to: LoveLetter, P.O. Box 313, Naperville, IL  60566
❧ Look for these books by "America's Romance Coach," Gregory J.P. Godek: *1001 Ways to Be Romantic*
*Romantic Mischief* ❧ *Romantic Fantasies* ❧ *Romantic Dates* ❧ *Romantic Questions*
❧ Check out the "World of Romance" page on the Internet: http://www.godek.com

# LOVE

### C O U P O N S

*This coupon entitles you to an evening of "Classic Romance." Included: The movie Casablanca; music by Glenn Miller; candlelight and champagne.*

*Personal notes* _____

_____

"Commitment requires daily renewal.
A promise kept, an action made, over and
over and over and over and over again."

-Gregory J.P. Godek, Author of *1001 Ways to Be Romantic*

Pick a number between 1 and
1001. This coupon entitles you to
choose any item from the book
*1001 Ways to Be Romantic.* If it's
affordable, the coupon-issuer will
fulfill the romantic idea described
in that number!

*Personal notes* _____

_____

"When a 'me' and a 'you' decide to become a couple, a new entity called 'Us' comes into being."

-Gregory J.P. Godek, Author of *1001 Ways to Be Romantic*

# LOVE

C O U P O N S

This coupon is good for one "choreographed" lovemaking session! Choose your favorite romantic/erotic music, and then make love to match its mood and rhythms.

*Personal notes* _____

_____

# "Romance is the environment in which love flourishes."

-Gregory J.P. Godek, Author of *1001 Ways to Be Romantic*

- Get a free 1 year subscription to Greg Godek's *LoveLetter Newsletter*.
  Send your name and address to: LoveLetter, P.O. Box 313, Naperville, IL 60566
- Look for these books by "America's Romance Coach," Gregory J.P. Godek: *1001 Ways to Be Romantic*
  *Romantic Mischief* ❧ *Romantic Fantasies* ❧ *Romantic Dates* ❧ *Romantic Questions*
- Check out the "World of Romance" page on the Internet: http://www.godek.com

**Nightgowns! Teddies!!
Stockings!!! Garter Belts!!!!
This coupon is good for a
$100 shopping spree in the
nearest lingerie shop (or
lingerie catalog). Shoppers
must be at least 18 years
of age.**

*Personal notes* _____

_____

> ## "To be loving is to be creative. To be creative is to express love."

-Gregory J.P. Godek, Author of *1001 Ways to Be Romantic*

- Get a free 1 year subscription to Greg Godek's *LoveLetter Newsletter*.
  Send your name and address to: LoveLetter, P.O. Box 313, Naperville, IL 60566
- Look for these books by "America's Romance Coach," Gregory J.P. Godek: *1001 Ways to Be Romantic*
  *Romantic Mischief* ❧ *Romantic Fantasies* ❧ *Romantic Dates* ❧ *Romantic Questions*
- Check out the "World of Romance" page on the Internet: http://www.godek.com

This is a *Saturday Night at the Movies* coupon. (Note: this is a "movie out date," not an "at home" video date.) Included: transportation, tickets, tub-o-popcorn, Milk Duds, soda.

*Personal notes* _____

_____

"Words express passion. Kissing confirms it."

-Gregory J.P. Godek, Author of *1001 Ways to Be Romantic*

L**O**VE

C O U P **O** N S

The classic, romantic,
Do-it-Yourself Coupon:

_____

_____

_____

_____

*Personal notes* _____

_____

"Romantic gestures have no ulterior motive.
Their only purpose is to express love."

-Gregory J.P. Godek, Author of *1001 Ways to Be Romantic*

LOVE

C O U P O N S

An Evening of
Dancing Coupon.
Kick up your heels for a
night on the town!

*Personal notes* _____

_____

# "A honeymoon is not a place– it's a state of mind."

-Gregory J.P. Godek, Author of *1001 Ways to Be Romantic*

# L♥VE

### C O U P O N S

*One romantic dinner at home.*
*Prepared by the coupon-issuer.*
*Proper dress required.*

*Personal notes* _____

_____

# "Romance is a process–it's not an event."

-Gregory J.P. Godek, Author of *1001 Ways to Be Romantic*

**Three wishes.** The coupon-giver will be your personal genie. "Your wish is my command!" (Wishes must be legal, affordable and physically possible to perform.)

*Personal notes* _____

_____

"Romance is the expression of love. It's the action step. It's bringing love alive in the world."

-Gregory J.P. Godek, Author of *1001 Ways to Be Romantic*

- Get a free 1 year subscription to Greg Godek's *LoveLetter Newsletter*.
  Send your name and address to: LoveLetter, P.O. Box 313, Naperville, IL  60566
- Look for these books by "America's Romance Coach," Gregory J.P. Godek: *1001 Ways to Be Romantic*
  *Romantic Mischief* ❧ *Romantic Fantasies* ❧ *Romantic Dates* ❧ *Romantic Questions*
- Check out the "World of Romance" page on the Internet: http://www.godek.com

# L♥VE
### C O U P O N S

**The Official Happy Birthday Coupon.**
In addition to providing you with a birthday cake, candles, balloons, streamers and a great surprise gift, the coupon issuer will happily sing "Happy Birthday to You."

*Personal notes* _____

_____

# "Ya' don't gotta be perfect–ya' just gotta keep tryin'!"

-Gregory J.P. Godek, Author of *1001 Ways to Be Romantic*

- Get a free 1 year subscription to Greg Godek's *LoveLetter Newsletter*.
  Send your name and address to: LoveLetter, P.O. Box 313, Naperville, IL 60566
- Look for these books by "America's Romance Coach," Gregory J.P. Godek: *1001 Ways to Be Romantic*
  *Romantic Mischief* *Romantic Fantasies* *Romantic Dates* *Romantic Questions*
- Check out the "World of Romance" page on the Internet: http://www.godek.com

*The Chocolate Kiss Coupon!*
*This coupon entitles you to (at least) 10*
*pounds of Hershey's Kisses. This coupon*
*supersedes any and all diets.*

*Personal notes* _____

_____

# "Lovers listen with their hearts."

-Gregory J.P. Godek, Author of *1001 Ways to Be Romantic*

**The Second Honeymoon Coupon!** You choose the type of vacation, your partner chooses the exact location. You choose the length of vacation, your partner chooses the departure date.
*Bon Voyage!*

*Personal notes* _____

_____

"Planning doesn't destroy spontaneity,
it creates opportunity."

-Gregory J.P. Godek, Author of *1001 Ways to Be Romantic*

# LOVE

C O U P O N S

The Official Valentine's Day Coupon. In addition to providing you with a heart-shaped box of chocolates and a dozen red roses, the coupon-issuer will treat you like the unique, special, wonderful person you are.

*Personal notes* _____

_____

"Consciously recommit yourself to your relationship every day."

-Gregory J.P. Godek, Author of *1001 Ways to Be Romantic*

**L♥VE**
C O U P O N S

This coupon entitles you to one
afternoon of window shopping
with the coupon giver.
Transportation and lunch are
included. Wishing and
dreaming are encouraged.
No purchases are necessary.

*Personal notes* _____

_____

"Lovers have an inner resource that takes them beyond the limits of what one person alone can achieve."

-Gregory J.P. Godek, Author of *1001 Ways to Be Romantic*

# L♡VE
### COUPONS

The Saturday Night Date Coupon. Where? Wherever you want. When? You decide. The coupon-giver guarantees a great time and will pay all expenses up to $75.00.

*Personal notes* _____

_____

"Intimacy is not required 24 hours a day. But it is required some time during every 24 hour period."

-Gregory J.P. Godek, Author of *1001 Ways to Be Romantic*

❧ Get a free 1 year subscription to Greg Godek's *LoveLetter Newsletter*.
  Send your name and address to: LoveLetter, P.O. Box 313, Naperville, IL  60566
❧ Look for these books by "America's Romance Coach," Gregory J.P. Godek: *1001 Ways to Be Romantic*
  *Romantic Mischief* ❧ *Romantic Fantasies* ❧ *Romantic Dates* ❧ *Romantic Questions*
❧ Check out the "World of Romance" page on the Internet: http://www.godek.com

**This is an "Expand Your Sexual Horizons" Coupon.** You get to ask the coupon-issuer to participate in a sexual activity that is slightly outrageous and/or positively scandalous.

*Personal notes* _____

_____

# "Take a classic romantic idea and give it a creative twist!"

-Gregory J.P. Godek, Author of *1001 Ways to Be Romantic*

- Get a free 1 year subscription to Greg Godek's *LoveLetter Newsletter*.
  Send your name and address to: LoveLetter, P.O. Box 313, Naperville, IL 60566
- Look for these books by "America's Romance Coach," Gregory J.P. Godek: *1001 Ways to Be Romantic Romantic Mischief* ❧ *Romantic Fantasies* ❧ *Romantic Dates* ❧ *Romantic Questions*
- Check out the "World of Romance" page on the Internet: http://www.godek.com

*This is a Couch Potato Coupon. It entitles you to a solid weekend of sitting in front of the TV, while the coupon-giver caters to all of your junk food needs.*

*Personal notes* _____

_____

"Because romantic moments are charged
with emotion, they create positive memories
that last a lifetime."

-Gregory J.P. Godek, Author of *1001 Ways to Be Romantic*

❧ Get a free 1 year subscription to Greg Godek's *LoveLetter* Newsletter.
Send your name and address to: LoveLetter, P.O. Box 313, Naperville, IL  60566
❧ Look for these books by "America's Romance Coach," Gregory J.P. Godek: *1001 Ways to Be Romantic*
*Romantic Mischief* ❧ *Romantic Fantasies* ❧ *Romantic Dates* ❧ *Romantic Questions*
❧ Check out the "World of Romance" page on the Internet: http://www.godek.com

**An All-Sports Weekend!**
The coupon-issuer will pay
for and accompany you to
any professional sporting
event taking place in your
vicinity within the
next month.

*Personal notes* _____

_____

# "You can be romantic without changing who you are."

-Gregory J.P. Godek, Author of *1001 Ways to Be Romantic*

❧ Get a free 1 year subscription to Greg Godek's *LoveLetter Newsletter*.
   Send your name and address to: LoveLetter, P.O. Box 313, Naperville, IL 60566
❧ Look for these books by "America's Romance Coach," Gregory J.P. Godek: *1001 Ways to Be Romantic*
   *Romantic Mischief* ❧ *Romantic Fantasies* ❧ *Romantic Dates* ❧ *Romantic Questions*
❧ Check out the "World of Romance" page on the Internet: http://www.godek.com

LOVE
C O U P O N S

*A "Coffee, Tea and Me" Coupon.*
*Good for coffee or tea*
*served to you anywhere*
*in your home, at a time*
*of your choosing.*

*Personal notes* _____

_____

# "Intimacy isn't simply an idea– it's an experience."

-Gregory J.P. Godek, Author of *1001 Ways to Be Romantic*

LOVE

C O U P O N S

*The Wacky "Half-Birthday"*
*Celebration Coupon! You are entitled to*
*celebrate your half-birthday—the day*
*exactly six months after your official*
*birthday. Included: cake and candles,*
*ice cream, and presents!*

*Personal notes* _____

_____

# "Do you have 20 years of experience–or one year of experience repeated 20 times?"

-Gregory J.P. Godek, Author of *1001 Ways to Be Romantic*

❧ Get a free 1 year subscription to Greg Godek's *LoveLetter Newsletter*.
  Send your name and address to: LoveLetter, P.O. Box 313, Naperville, IL  60566
❧ Look for these books by "America's Romance Coach," Gregory J.P. Godek: *1001 Ways to Be Romantic*
  *Romantic Mischief* ❧ *Romantic Fantasies* ❧ *Romantic Dates* ❧ *Romantic Questions*
❧ Check out the "World of Romance" page on the Internet: http://www.godek.com

LOVE

C O U P O N S

**The Sweets-for-the-Sweet Coupon.** You are entitled to an eleven-pound pile of any three kinds of candy that you specify. Poundage of the pile must be verified by an independent third party.

*Personal notes* _____

_____

# "Become an artist of your relationship."

-Gregory J.P. Godek, Author of *1001 Ways to Be Romantic*

# LOVE

C O U P O N S

This coupon entitles you to a Weekend Movie Marathon. You choose a theme, and the coupon-issuer will rent six to eight movies that fit the theme, pop the popcorn and be your weekend movie date.

*Personal notes* _____

_____

"Intimate communication takes place heart-to-heart."

-Gregory J.P. Godek, Author of *1001 Ways to Be Romantic*

# L♥VE

## C O U P O N S

A "Quickie" Coupon.
This rare and highly-prized
coupon entitles you to sex
with the coupon-giver
*immediately* upon you
handing this coupon back
to him or her. No excuses
accepted.

*Personal notes* _____

_____

# "Romance is the language of love."

-Gregory J.P. Godek, Author of *1001 Ways to Be Romantic*

# L♡VE

### C O U P O N S

*This coupon entitles you to a day of "Kissin'-un'-a-Lovin'"! (If you need directions for this one, you need more help than a mere coupon can provide!)*

*Personal notes* _____

_____

"Celebrate your similarities.
Honor your differences."

-Gregory J.P. Godek, Author of *1001 Ways to Be Romantic*

※ Get a free 1 year subscription to Greg Godek's *LoveLetter Newsletter*.
  Send your name and address to: LoveLetter, P.O. Box 313, Naperville, IL 60566
※ Look for these books by "America's Romance Coach," Gregory J.P. Godek: *1001 Ways to Be Romantic*
  *Romantic Mischief* ※ *Romantic Fantasies* ※ *Romantic Dates* ※ *Romantic Questions*
※ Check out the "World of Romance" page on the Internet: http://www.godek.com

C O U P O N S

A **"Fantasy Island" Coupon,** in which the coupon giver agrees to play along with any sexual fantasy your fertile imagination can come up with. Not voided by any decency laws whatsoever.

*Personal notes* _____

_____

"Go above and beyond. Do the unexpected. Give more than you have to."

-Gregory J.P. Godek, Author of *1001 Ways to Be Romantic*

❧ Get a free 1 year subscription to Greg Godek's *LoveLetter* Newsletter.
  Send your name and address to: LoveLetter, P.O. Box 313, Naperville, IL 60566
❧ Look for these books by "America's Romance Coach," Gregory J.P. Godek: *1001 Ways to Be Romantic*
  *Romantic Mischief* ❧ *Romantic Fantasies* ❧ *Romantic Dates* ❧ *Romantic Questions*
❧ Check out the "World of Romance" page on the Internet: http://www.godek.com

**LOVE**

C O U P O N S

An Ice Cream Sundae Coupon.
The coupon-issuer will
supply the ice cream, hot fudge,
peanuts, bananas and other
toppings. You supply the creativity.
This coupon includes a one hour
reprieve from any diets.

*Personal notes* _____

_____

# "Great relationships change, grow and evolve."

-Gregory J.P. Godek, Author of *1001 Ways to Be Romantic*

- ✸ Get a free 1 year subscription to Greg Godek's *LoveLetter Newsletter*.
  Send your name and address to: LoveLetter, P.O. Box 313, Naperville, IL 60566
- ✸ Look for these books by "America's Romance Coach," Gregory J.P. Godek: *1001 Ways to Be Romantic*
  *Romantic Mischief* ✸ *Romantic Fantasies* ✸ *Romantic Dates* ✸ *Romantic Questions*
- ✸ Check out the "World of Romance" page on the Internet: http://www.godek.com

A Cuddle Coupon.
Good for 2 hours of cuddling
with the coupon-issuer in one of
the following locations: in front
of a roaring fire, on a porch
swing, on a cozy couch, or in a
bed. TV is prohibited. Radio
is permitted.

*Personal notes* _____

_____

"Love does not–cannot–hurt. It's the absence of love that hurts."

-Gregory J.P. Godek, Author of *1001 Ways to Be Romantic*

- ✤ Get a free 1 year subscription to Greg Godek's *LoveLetter Newsletter*.
  Send your name and address to: LoveLetter, P.O. Box 313, Naperville, IL 60566
- ✤ Look for these books by "America's Romance Coach," Gregory J.P. Godek: *1001 Ways to Be Romantic*
  *Romantic Mischief* ✤ *Romantic Fantasies* ✤ *Romantic Dates* ✤ *Romantic Questions*
- ✤ Check out the "World of Romance" page on the Internet: http://www.godek.com

# L♥VE

## C O U P O N S

You are invited to a "Quickie Picnic." The coupon-issuer will provide the wine, crackers and cheese, blanket, transportation and fascinating conversation. Duration: 2 to 3 hours.

*Personal notes* _____

_____

# "Turn the ordinary into the special."

-Gregory J.P. Godek, Author of *1001 Ways to Be Romantic*

❧ Get a free 1 year subscription to Greg Godek's *LoveLetter Newsletter*.
  Send your name and address to: LoveLetter, P.O. Box 313, Naperville, IL  60566
❧ Look for these books by "America's Romance Coach," Gregory J.P. Godek: *1001 Ways to Be Romantic*
  *Romantic Mischief* ❧ *Romantic Fantasies* ❧ *Romantic Dates* ❧ *Romantic Questions*
❧ Check out the "World of Romance" page on the Internet: http://www.godek.com

LOVE
C O U P O N S

**The Ultimate Picnic Coupon. This coupon entitles you to an all-out, elegant, dinner picnic. Included: 3 course meal, fine wine, candles and music. Proper dress required.**

*Personal notes* _____

_____

"Time is your most precious commodity.
You give yourself when you give your time."

-Gregory J.P. Godek, Author of *1001 Ways to Be Romantic*

**L♥VE**

C O U P O N S

*Happy Anniversary!*
*You are entitled to a day of True*
*Togetherness. This means a day just for*
*the two of you: no kids, no job, no*
*responsibilities, no chores.*

*Personal notes* _____

_____

"If your relationship were a painting, what would it look like?"

-Gregory J.P. Godek, Author of *1001 Ways to Be Romantic*

❧ Get a free 1 year subscription to Greg Godek's *LoveLetter Newsletter*.
   Send your name and address to: LoveLetter, P.O. Box 313, Naperville, IL  60566
❧ Look for these books by "America's Romance Coach," Gregory J.P. Godek: *1001 Ways to Be Romantic*
   *Romantic Mischief* ❧ *Romantic Fantasies* ❧ *Romantic Dates* ❧ *Romantic Questions*
❧ Check out the "World of Romance" page on the Internet: http://www.godek.com

# LOVE
### C O U P O N S

A Lazy Love Coupon.
This one-of-a-kind coupon
entitles you to a sensuous,
luxurious, extended lovemaking
session with the coupon-issuer.
Time requirement: At least 3 hours.

*Personal notes* _____

_____

"In what direction is your passion pointing you?  Follow it!"

-Gregory J.P. Godek, Author of *1001 Ways to Be Romantic*

**LOVE**

**C O U P O N S**

Jewelry, Jewelry, Jewelry!
This amazing coupon is
redeemable at any jewelry
store anywhere in the world.
Good for a truly outrageous
purchase. You choose your
gift. The coupon-issuer pays
the bill. Up to
$_____.

*Personal notes* _____

_____

"Give your lover 15 minutes of undivided attention every day."

-Gregory J.P. Godek, Author of *1001 Ways to Be Romantic*

The Ultimate, Fantastic, Delicious Pizza Coupon. Good for one date at the best pizza joint in town. (Ask the chef to place the pepperoni in the shape of a heart.)

*Personal notes* _____

"Great relationships require equal parts of passion, commitment and intimacy."

-Gregory J.P. Godek, Author of *1001 Ways to Be Romantic*

# L♡VE

### C O U P O N S

*This coupon is redeemable for one bottle of fine wine. Also included: one romantic setting in which to enjoy the wine.*

*Personal notes* _____

_____

# "Avoid generic gifts."

-Gregory J.P. Godek, Author of *1001 Ways to Be Romantic*

- Get a free 1 year subscription to Greg Godek's *LoveLetter Newsletter*.
  Send your name and address to: LoveLetter, P.O. Box 313, Naperville, IL  60566
- Look for these books by "America's Romance Coach," Gregory J.P. Godek: *1001 Ways to Be Romantic*
  *Romantic Mischief* ❧ *Romantic Fantasies* ❧ *Romantic Dates* ❧ *Romantic Questions*
- Check out the "World of Romance" page on the Internet: http://www.godek.com

**L⊙VE**

C O U P O N S

The Romantic Movie Coupon.
Choose one: *Out of Africa,
Casablanca, Ghost, Somewhere
in Time, Splendor in the Grass,
Sleepless in Seattle, Top Hat,
Tootsie, Key Largo,
Moonstruck, When Harry
Met Sally.*

*Personal notes* _____

_____

> "Intimacy isn't simply an idea–
> it's an experience."

-Gregory J.P. Godek, Author of *1001 Ways to Be Romantic*

# L♡VE
## COUPONS

*Personal notes* _____

The *Joy of Sex Coupon!*
The coupon-giver
provides the book. You
choose the page. You
both enjoy yourselves
and each other as you
follow the instructions
on that page.

# "Money can't buy you love...but it can buy you a little romance!"

-Gregory J.P. Godek, Author of *1001 Ways to Be Romantic*

- Get a free 1 year subscription to Greg Godek's *LoveLetter Newsletter*.
  Send your name and address to: LoveLetter, P.O. Box 313, Naperville, IL 60566
- Look for these books by "America's Romance Coach," Gregory J.P. Godek: *1001 Ways to Be Romantic* *Romantic Mischief* *Romantic Fantasies* *Romantic Dates* *Romantic Questions*
- Check out the "World of Romance" page on the Internet: http://www.godek.com

LOVE

C O U P O N S

*This coupon entitles you to a "Quickie Back Massage" performed by the coupon-giver. Must be performed immediately upon relinquishment of this coupon. Maximum time limit: 7 minutes.*

*Personal notes* _____

_____

# "Celebrate *something* every month."

-Gregory J.P. Godek, Author of *1001 Ways to Be Romantic*

- Get a free 1 year subscription to Greg Godek's *LoveLetter Newsletter*.
  Send your name and address to: LoveLetter, P.O. Box 313, Naperville, IL 60566
- Look for these books by "America's Romance Coach," Gregory J.P. Godek: *1001 Ways to Be Romantic*
  *Romantic Mischief* ❧ *Romantic Fantasies* ❧ *Romantic Dates* ❧ *Romantic Questions*
- Check out the "World of Romance" page on the Internet: http://www.godek.com

The Ultimate Full-Body Massage: The coupon-issuer will give you a one-hour, professional-style, full-body massage. Complete with scented oil. Coupon-issuer is required to study a book on massage techniques.

*Personal notes* _____

_____

# "Romance is expressing your feelings in your way."

-Gregory J.P. Godek, Author of *1001 Ways to Be Romantic*

❧ Get a free 1 year subscription to Greg Godek's *LoveLetter Newsletter*.
Send your name and address to: LoveLetter, P.O. Box 313, Naperville, IL  60566
❧ Look for these books by "America's Romance Coach," Gregory J.P. Godek: *1001 Ways to Be Romantic*
*Romantic Mischief* ❧ *Romantic Fantasies* ❧ *Romantic Dates* ❧ *Romantic Questions*
❧ Check out the "World of Romance" page on the Internet: http://www.godek.com

**L♥VE**

C  O  U  P  O  N  S

Happy Anniversary! You are entitled to choose one of the following: 1) Dinner for two, 2) A romantic movie date, 3) An awesome backrub, or 4) A sexy lovemaking session.

*Personal notes* _____

_____

> "The anticipation is often as much fun
> as the gift or gesture itself."

-Gregory J.P. Godek, Author of *1001 Ways to Be Romantic*

- Get a free 1 year subscription to Greg Godek's *LoveLetter Newsletter*.
  Send your name and address to: LoveLetter, P.O. Box 313, Naperville, IL 60566
- Look for these books by "America's Romance Coach," Gregory J.P. Godek: *1001 Ways to Be Romantic*
  *Romantic Mischief* ❧ *Romantic Fantasies* ❧ *Romantic Dates* ❧ *Romantic Questions*
- Check out the "World of Romance" page on the Internet: http://www.godek.com

**LOVE COUPONS**

*This coupon entitles you to either an afternoon of watching clouds, or a night of watching shooting stars.*

*Personal notes* _____

_____

# "Great relationships aren't 50/50– they're 100/100."

-Gregory J.P. Godek, Author of *1001 Ways to Be Romantic*

- Get a free 1 year subscription to Greg Godek's *LoveLetter Newsletter*.
  Send your name and address to: LoveLetter, P.O. Box 313, Naperville, IL 60566
- Look for these books by "America's Romance Coach," Gregory J.P. Godek: *1001 Ways to Be Romantic*
  *Romantic Mischief* ❧ *Romantic Fantasies* ❧ *Romantic Dates* ❧ *Romantic Questions*
- Check out the "World of Romance" page on the Internet: http://www.godek.com

**LOVE**

C O U P O N S

One Carnival Coupon. Good for a full afternoon of rides on the roller coaster, tilt-a-whirl, ferris wheel or merry-go-round. Includes all the popcorn, peanuts, pizza, cotton candy and candy apples you can eat!

*Personal notes* _____

_____

# "Romance is 'Adult Play.'"

-Gregory J.P. Godek, Author of *1001 Ways to Be Romantic*

**LOVE**
C O U P O N S

The Half-Day-Off-Work Coupon. You specify the day. The coupon-giver will arrange with your employer for a half a day off work for you. He or she will also arrange a romantic surprise activity for you.

*Personal notes* _____

_____

"Love is more than just a feeling.  It is a lifelong journey of self-discovery. "

-Gregory J.P. Godek, Author of *1001 Ways to Be Romantic*

❧ Get a free 1 year subscription to Greg Godek's *LoveLetter Newsletter*.
  Send your name and address to: LoveLetter, P.O. Box 313, Naperville, IL  60566
❧ Look for these books by "America's Romance Coach," Gregory J.P. Godek: *1001 Ways to Be Romantic Romantic Mischief* ❧ *Romantic Fantasies* ❧ *Romantic Dates* ❧ *Romantic Questions*
❧ Check out the "World of Romance" page on the Internet: http://www.godek.com

*The Decadent Dinner-In-Bed Coupon. Forget breakfast in bed—you're being treated to an elegant dinner in bed sometime in the next week! (Make sure to save time for "dessert"!)*

*Personal notes* _____

_____

"Love. Don't waste precious time trying to *define* it. Spend your time *experiencing* it!"

-Gregory J.P. Godek, Author of *1001 Ways to Be Romantic*

**LOVE**

C O U P O N S

The first ever "Second Valentine's Day of the Year" Coupon. Yes, this coupon allows you to celebrate a second Valentine's Day on a day of your choosing! Complete with roses, chocolates, cards, etc.

*Personal notes* _____

_____

"Through your intimate relationship, you and your partner experience the beginnings of Oneness."

-Gregory J.P. Godek, Author of *1001 Ways to Be Romantic*

❧ Get a free 1 year subscription to Greg Godek's *LoveLetter Newsletter*.
   Send your name and address to: LoveLetter, P.O. Box 313, Naperville, IL  60566
❧ Look for these books by "America's Romance Coach," Gregory J.P. Godek: *1001 Ways to Be Romantic*
   *Romantic Mischief* ❧ *Romantic Fantasies* ❧ *Romantic Dates* ❧ *Romantic Questions*
❧ Check out the "World of Romance" page on the Internet: http://www.godek.com

L♡VE

C O U P O N S

This coupon entitles you
to one make-out session
at you local Lover's Lane.
The coupon-issuer is
responsible for providing
a car with a roomy
back seat.

*Personal notes* _____

_____

# "Don't coast! Relationships in Neutral end-up in Reverse!"

-Gregory J.P. Godek, Author of *1001 Ways to Be Romantic*

ॐ Get a free 1 year subscription to Greg Godek's *LoveLetter Newsletter*.
   Send your name and address to: LoveLetter, P.O. Box 313, Naperville, IL  60566
ॐ Look for these books by "America's Romance Coach," Gregory J.P. Godek: *1001 Ways to Be Romantic*
   *Romantic Mischief* ॐ *Romantic Fantasies* ॐ *Romantic Dates* ॐ *Romantic Questions*
ॐ Check out the "World of Romance" page on the Internet: http://www.godek.com

LOVE
C O U P O N S

*This coupon entitles you to one evening of stimulation. You define what kind of "stimulation" you want, and the coupon-giver will supply it. You may choose intellectual stimulation—or the more physical kind!*

Personal notes _____
_____

# "Treat your anniversaries as 'Personal Holidays.'"

-Gregory J.P. Godek, Author of *1001 Ways to Be Romantic*

- Get a free 1 year subscription to Greg Godek's *LoveLetter Newsletter*.
  Send your name and address to: LoveLetter, P.O. Box 313, Naperville, IL 60566
- Look for these books by "America's Romance Coach," Gregory J.P. Godek: *1001 Ways to Be Romantic Romantic Mischief* • *Romantic Fantasies* • *Romantic Dates* • *Romantic Questions*
- Check out the "World of Romance" page on the Internet: http://www.godek.com

One Romantic Dinner at home. Prepared by the coupon-issuer. Proper dress required.

*Personal notes* _____

_____

"Your shared experiences and joint memories weave a tapestry that combines your two into one."

-Gregory J.P. Godek, Author of *1001 Ways to Be Romantic*

**LOVE**

C O U P O N S

The Chocoholic Coupon.
You are entitled to a massive,
no-holds-barred celebration
of chocolate! Included: an
extraordinary amount of
chocolate and all your
favorite brands.

*Personal notes* _____

_____

# "It's the meaning that matters, not the words."

-Gregory J.P. Godek, Author of *1001 Ways to Be Romantic*

❧ Get a free 1 year subscription to Greg Godek's *LoveLetter Newsletter*.
   Send your name and address to: LoveLetter, P.O. Box 313, Naperville, IL 60566
❧ Look for these books by "America's Romance Coach," Gregory J.P. Godek: *1001 Ways to Be Romantic*
   *Romantic Mischief* ❧ *Romantic Fantasies* ❧ *Romantic Dates* ❧ *Romantic Questions*
❧ Check out the "World of Romance" page on the Internet: http://www.godek.com

**L** ♥ **VE**

**C O U P O N S**

*This coupon entitles you to 3 full hours of uninterrupted peace and quiet. You get to choose the time. The coupon-issuer is responsible for the removal of all distractions.*

*Personal notes* _____

_____

# "Treat your partner like your best friend as well as lover."

-Gregory J.P. Godek, Author of *1001 Ways to Be Romantic*

- Get a free 1 year subscription to Greg Godek's *LoveLetter Newsletter*.
  Send your name and address to: LoveLetter, P.O. Box 313, Naperville, IL 60566
- Look for these books by "America's Romance Coach," Gregory J.P. Godek: *1001 Ways to Be Romantic*
  *Romantic Mischief* ◆ *Romantic Fantasies* ◆ *Romantic Dates* ◆ *Romantic Questions*
- Check out the "World of Romance" page on the Internet: http://www.godek.com

L♡VE

C O U P ♡ N S

The "Sleep-In-Late" Coupon.
You are entitled to sleep 'til
noon! Simply remit this
coupon to the issuer with 24
hours notice, and he or she will
be responsible for the removal
of all noise or other
annoyances.

*Personal notes* _____

_____

# "A marriage license is not a license to change your partner."

-Gregory J.P. Godek, Author of *1001 Ways to Be Romantic*

- ❧ Get a free 1 year subscription to Greg Godek's *LoveLetter Newsletter*.
  Send your name and address to: LoveLetter, P.O. Box 313, Naperville, IL 60566
- ❧ Look for these books by "America's Romance Coach," Gregory J.P. Godek: *1001 Ways to Be Romantic*
  *Romantic Mischief* ❧ *Romantic Fantasies* ❧ *Romantic Dates* ❧ *Romantic Questions*
- ❧ Check out the "World of Romance" page on the Internet: http://www.godek.com

**The Bubblebath-For-Two Coupon.**
**You know what to do.**
**Void where prohibited by tiny size of tub.**

*Personal notes* _____

_____

"With practice, romance becomes as natural and all-pervasive as breathing."

-Gregory J.P. Godek, Author of *1001 Ways to Be Romantic*

- ❧ Get a free 1 year subscription to Greg Godek's *LoveLetter Newsletter*.
  Send your name and address to: LoveLetter, P.O. Box 313, Naperville, IL 60566
- ❧ Look for these books by "America's Romance Coach," Gregory J.P. Godek: *1001 Ways to Be Romantic*
  *Romantic Mischief* ❧ *Romantic Fantasies* ❧ *Romantic Dates* ❧ *Romantic Questions*
- ❧ Check out the "World of Romance" page on the Internet: http://www.godek.com

**Yes!** Sign me up for a free one-year subscription to Greg Godek's LoveLetter Newsletter.

Name:_____

Address: _____

City:_____ State: _____ Zip: _____

Send to:
LoveLetter
Sourcebooks
P.O. Box 313
Naperville, IL  60566

## My Ideas

Other books in this series include:

Romantic Dates: Ways to Woo & Wow the One You Love          ISBN: 1-57071-153-4; $6.95
Romantic Fantasies: & Other Sexy Ways of Expressing Your Love     ISBN: 1-57071-154-2; $6.95
Romantic Mischief: The Playful Side of Love                ISBN: 1-57071-151-8; $6.95
Romantic Questions: Growing Closer Through Intimate Conversation   ISBN: 1-57071-152-6; $6.95

*And don't miss the classic:*
1001 Ways to Be Romantic                          ISBN: 1-883518-05-9; $14.95

To order these books or any other of our many publications, please contact your local bookseller, gift store or call Sourcebooks. Books by Gregory J.P. Godek are available in book and gift stores across North America. Get a copy of our catalog by writing or faxing:

Sourcebooks
P. O. Box 372
Naperville, IL  60566
(630) 961-3900
FAX: (630) 961-2168

Other great coupon books from Sourcebooks

I Love You Mom Coupons
I Love You Dad Coupons
Golf Coupons
The Best of Friends Coupons
The Chocoholic's Coupon Book
Happy Birthday Coupons
My Favorite Teacher Coupons
Merry Christmas Coupons

These titles and other Sourcebooks publications are available now at your local book or gift store, or by calling Sourcebooks at (630) 961-3900.